Cromosys Publication

Teach Yourself German

NIRANJAN JHA SHOWMAN

Founder - Niranjan Jha Showman

Education and Technology Research Center

Patankar Park, Nallasopara (W), Mumbai. +91-9561450045

Education, Technology, Publication, Healthcare, Newsmedia, Realtor, Filmmaking

www.facebook.com/cromosys

+91-9561450045
Learn Advanced Skills
And Get Job Instantly
GERMAN
Python
FRENCH
C++
SPANISH
Java
ENGLISH
HTML5
RUSSIAN
CSS
JavaScript
Cromosys
Education and Technology Research Center
Nallasopara (W), Mumbai

Learn Web Programming
Demo-Class Free
HTML
CSS
React
JavaScript
Typescript
Bootstrap
Cromosys
20 Years of Experience
Nallasopara (W), Mumbai
+91-9561450045

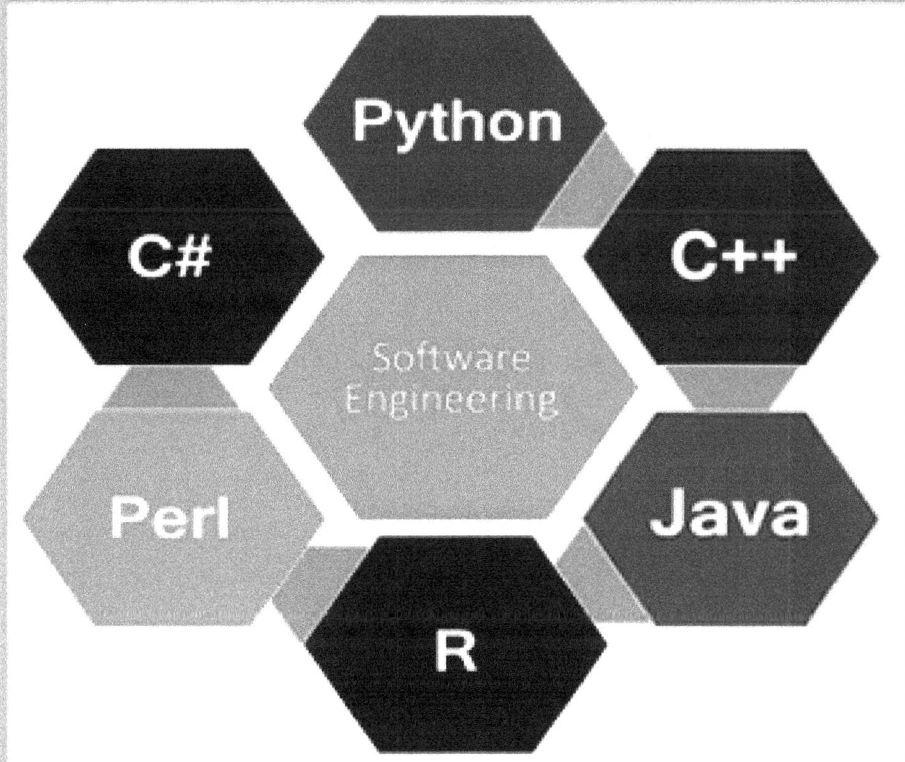

+91-9561450045
Learn Software Engineering
Demo-Class Free
Python
C#
C++
Software Engineering
Perl
Java
R
Cromosys
20 Years of Experience
Nallasopara (W), Mumbai
+91-9561450045

25 Years of Experience
Learn Visual Multimedia
Animation VFX
Movie Editing
Game Development
Cromosys
+91-9561450045
Education and Technology Research Center
Nallasopara (W), Mumbai
www.facebook.com/cromosys

Jobs Available
For Candidates Who Know

German
French
Spanish

Vacancy in Germany, France, Spain

For Hospitality, Engineering, IT Sector
With Free Visa, Airfare and Accommodation

Cromosys

Education and Technology Research Centre
Nallasopara (W), Mumbai
+91-9561450045
20 Years of Experience

+91-9561450045
Foreign Languages Institute
German, French, Spanish
Basic and Advanced - All Levels
3 x 6 = 18 Courses
FRANCHISE
Business Offer
Teaching Materials Provided
We have 1 Million Students Globally
Great Income Assured
Global Exposure
Cromosys
20 Years of Experience
Nallasopara (W), Mumbai
+91-9561450045

Cromosys Publication

Teach Yourself German

Niranjan Jha Showman

"Education taken with zeal educes to success."
~Niranjan Showman

Preface

Cromosys Publication's "Teach Yourself German" book is an optimal quality guide to the beginners as well as advanced learners. German is the language of great demand after English as it is widely spoken in many European countries. Language is the pillar of human origin and evolution, and so, even many other languages of the world died in this century, but German is still surviving and flourishing because of its strong root in human culture and civilization. Moreover, the grammar of German language is the base of English grammar too. This book is unmatchable and unique of its kind that guarantees your success. The lessons and study materials exclusively designed are based on my fifteen years of research in linguistic field. The text, audio and video are magnificently powerful to bring you into educational light. Whether your intention is to work, travel abroad or plunge deep into your research, if you need to learn a language, then German is the best choice.

Around eight years ago, when I went to the USA, I got a chance to learn it, and since then I have been teaching this language globally with high exposure. Having been communicating with German-speaking people around the world while managing a team in several call centers, and being able to understand linguistic science, I would like to assure you that this language is easy to learn in just one moth of daily practice. And once learnt, with your sharpened bilingual ability, you can make your way of success without any hindrance. After you start the lesson of this book, you don't need to worry about anything but just follow each and every lesson carefully. Don't procrastinate and never give up. You are going to do the most beautiful thing for yourself, so be bold enough to complete all the lessons. The sentence constructions of German are similar to English, only a few things which are not similar, I have explained properly in the easiest method I could ever find. The pronunciation of each word is given in bracket to help you speak correctly.

The significance of this book is that it is dynamic, systemic and blissful with abundance of pure and perfect set of rules that took a decade of time in preparation. One being immaturely suggested, spends ages in watching movies and listening to the audio in lure of learning German. But it doesn't bring success as they imitate a little but don't learn what in actual sense German is. And their never-ending process of Picasso Adventure collects some scattered information which is unworthy to learning a foreign language. So the aspirants get lost in wilderness. You may have seen some other books on German full of conversations and dialogues which the students purchase by mistake, but they quit learning soon because those are not the proper books. Just memorizing the dialogues will not take you anywhere. So I have designed this book with proper set of lessons to make you start your adventure sitting at home beginning with real basic. This book is highly useful for people working in communication based industry, media houses, entertainment world, and for those who are teachers, writers, researchers and students. And definitely for those who love languages – especially German!

Cromosys, our education and technology research center, saving human efforts from being wasted, is dedicated to teach you this language as good as possible. The world growing with density has brought enormous opportunity to foreign language speakers irrespective of their geographical boundaries. Having been teaching this language from several years, I have come across numerous unique rules which I have elaborated and explained in this book. Our path-breaking pioneer training institute, Cromosys, is committed to enlightening human mind with educational endeavors, and we are doing the same from fifteen successful years. I believe I have done all that I could to make this book useful to you, and not only hopeful but I am sure that your success is in your hand now because this book will take you miles ahead in your expectation. We always respect the views and comments of readers, so for any communication with regards to assistance, enquiry or collaboration, we are always at your reach as it helps us improve our ability.

Niranjan Jha Showman
Trainer, Author Physician, Entrepreneur, Filmmaker, Activist
Founder of Cromosys Corporation
facebook.com/cromosys
+91-9561450045
cromosys@yahoo.com
Nallasopara (W), Mumbai, India

My other books: -
English Voice Accent and Pronunciation
Teach Yourself German
Teach Yourself French
Teach Yourself Spanish
Be millionaire like me
Dynamic Grammar of English
Teach Yourself HTML5
Teach Yourself 3ds Max
Teach Yourself Autodesk Maya

Cromosys Corporation
Education and Technology Research Center
Education, Technology, Publication, Healthcare, Realtor, Filmmaking
facebook.com/cromosys
+91-9561450045
cromosys@yahoo.com
Nallasopara (W), Mumbai, India

About the Author

Niranjan Jha Showman
Trainer, Author, Physician, Entrepreneur, Filmmaker, Activist

Niranjan Jha Showman is a Language Scientist and Technical Researcher. He is the Award Winning author of more than fifty educational and fictional books at Amazon. He is one of the great-grandsons of the first President of India Dr. Rajendra Prasad. He is a Public Figure, and the globally - renowned Languages Trainer of French, Spanish, and German from past twenty years. Niranjan Jha Showman is an Entrepreneur and also works as a Filmmaker in India. Being the founder and owner of Cromosys Corporation - a company located in Mumbai, India, his company is excelling in the fields of Education, Technology, Publication, Newsmedia, Realtors, Banking, and Cinemascope from past fifteen years.

Niranjan Jha Showman's good-seller educational books and novels are appreciated worldwide. He has more than one million eBook buyers online, and more than one million learners are connected to him globally. One of his novels is critically acclaimed. He is the trainer of French, Spanish, German, English Voice and Accent, and Advanced Computer Education. He is also a political activist in India.

Niranjan Jha Showman is the man who came from rags to riches, he who knows how to turn the table, and he, whom you call the man of Midas-touch. He has observed lives from the Pandora of monkeys to the sanctuary of monks, not only down-to-earth but down-to-grave. He is a B. Com. graduate, and B. Ed. from Delhi University, and diploma holder in French, Spanish and German from America. You can watch his songs, movies, educational videos and many more things by typing "Niranjan Jha Showman" in Google.

Niranjan Jha Showman
+91-9561450045
cromosys@yahoo.com
Mumbai, India
facebook.com/cromosys

Statutory

This book with its content is the registered property of the author Niranjan Jha Showman.
The author and his Cromosys Publication holds all necessary rights of this book.
The copyright certificate of this book is attached at the end of this book.

This book is a copyright and its content is the registered property of the author Niranjan Jha Showman. The author and his Cromosys Publication holds all necessary rights of this book. All the writing works that include all the educational, non-educational books, novels, and articles of the writer Niranjan Jha Showman, are the registered content under MAHENG12112/13/1/2009-TC and the endorsement no. 3244 28/5/2009 with the Ministry of Information and Broadcasting, Govt. of India. Any plagiarism in this regard will attract strict legal action. Any further publication or production of any of his books requires his written permission. The copyright certificate of this book is attached at the end of this book.

Lesson 1
Alphabet

There are 26 letters in German alphabet. All are same as of English. Next to each letter the pronunciation is given. Write the letters in your notebook and speak out the pronunciation for practice. Don't jump up to the next lesson without proper practice of this lesson.

A	aa
B	bay (b+e)
C	tsay (t+s+e)
D	day
E	ay (ei)
F	eff
G	gay (g+e)
H	haa
I	ee
J	yot
K	kaa
L	el
M	em
N	en
O	o
P	pay
Q	koo
R	err
S	es
T	tay (t+e)
U	oo
V	fow
W	way (w+e)
X	iks
Y	ipselon
Z	tset (t+s+e+t)

* J is pronounced 'yot' in Germany but 'ye' in Austria.

* U is pronounced with 'round closed lips'.

* R is pronounced like guttural (in throat) = 'r+h'.

Lesson 2
Pronunciation

This lesson explains the proper pronunciation of the letters and lists the example words with their pronunciation also. You are required to concentrate more because you may find some pronunciation quite strange.

All the nouns MUST begin with a capital letter and other words with a small letter.

A – It is generally pronounced as 'aa' in a word.
kalt (kaalt) = cold
rosa (rozaa) = pink

B – This letter is pronounced same as in English.
Bruder (brooder) = brother
sieben (zeeben) = seven

When 'b' comes at the end of a word, it is pronounced like 'p'.
derb (derp) = strong
oberhalb (oberhaalp) = above

C – It usually sounds 'k', but 'ch' sounds – heavy 'kh'.
campen (kaampen) = to camp
cremig (kremish) = creamy (ending 'g' sounds 'sh'.

When 'ch' comes after a, o, u, it sounds 'kh'.
auch (aaukh) = also
nach (naakh) = after

When 'ch' comes after i, e, l, it sounds 'sh'.
Milch (milsh) = milk
ich (ish) = I

D – It is pronounced same as in English.
Dame (daame) = lady, woman
Dorf (dawrf) = village

If 'd' comes at the end of a word, it sounds 't'.
Feld (felt) = field
Kind (kint) = child

E – It is pronounced like 'e'.
Tante (taante) = aunt
Birne (birne) = bulb

Lesson 3
Pronunciation

F – This letter is pronounced same as in English.
Freund (froi-ent) = frined
Ehefrau (ehefraw) = wife

G – This letter is pronounced same as English.
Gefahr (gefaar) = danger
August (aaugust) = August

If 'g' comes at the end of a word after 'i' like 'ig', then 'g' is pronounced like 'sh'.
wenig (wenish) – little
ledig (ledish) = unmarried

If 'g' comes after 'a', and at the end of a word, then 'g' is pronounced like 'k'.
Tag (taak) = day

Sometimes the ending 'g' is also pronounced like 'k'.
Liebling (leeplink) = darling

H – It sounds same as in English.
Haar (haar) = hair
Huhn (hoon) = chicken

If 'h' comes in the middle of a word after a vowel, then 'h' remains silent.
Ehemann (ehemaan) = husband
lahm (laam) = lame

I – It is pronounced like 'ee' or small 'i'.
dieser (deezer) = this
ihr (eer) = yours

J – This letter is pronounced like 'y'.
Juli (yooli) = July
ja (yaa) = yes

K – It sounds same as in English.
kaufen (kawfen) = to buy

L – It sounds same as in English.
hohl (hol) = hollow or empty

Lesson 4
Pronunciation

M – This letter sounds same as in English.
Milch (milsh) = milk

N – This letter sounds same as in English.
Nabel (naabel) = navel
Nichte (nishte) = niece
Neffe (nefe) = nephew

O – This letter sounds same as in English 'o' or 'aw'.
Ofen (ofen) = stove
toll (tol) = great
Obst (opst) = fruit

P – This letter sounds same as in English.
Pack (paak) = packet
Oper (oper) = opera

Q – It is always pronounced like 'ku' because it comes with the letter u as – 'qu'.
Qual (kuaal) = agony

R – This letter with 'r' sound is rolled up – 'r+h'.
rot (rot) = red

S – It sounds 's' if it comes in the beginning or at the end of a word.
das (daas) = this
Glas (glaas) = glass
bis (bis) = till

When a vowel falls after 's', then it is pronounced like 'z'.
Esel (ezel) = donkey
Hose (hoze) = trousers
seit (zaa-it) = since

T – It is pronounced same as English.
Mutter (muter) = mother
Tabak (tabaak) = tobacco
Salat (zalaat) = salad
Hotel (hotel) = hotel

Lesson 5
Pronunciation

U – It is pronounced like 'oo' or 'u'.
Hut (hoot) = hat
gut (goot) = good
blau (blaau) = blue
Suppe (zoope) = soup
und (unt) = and

V – This letter sounds like 'f'.
Vater (faater) = father
voll (fawl) = full
Vetter (feter) cousin brother
viel (feel) = much

In some Greek and Latin words adopted in German, 'v' is pronounced like 'v'.
vage (vaage) = vague
November (november) = November

W – This letter sounds same as in English.
wenn (wen) = when, if
Wasser (waaser) = water
Wort (wort) = word
wahr (waar) = true

X – It sounds same as in English.
Taxi (taaksi) = taxi

Y – It is pronounced like 'y' of English.
Yacht (jaakht) = yacht

Z – It is pronounced like soft 'ts' which is a combined sound of 't+s'.
Zwerg (tswerk) = dwarf
zehnte (tsente) = tenth
Zwiebel (tsveebel) = onion
Zitrone (tseetrone) = lemon

Strict Instructions

Remember that learning German is never difficult. The only thing you have to do is that take this book as a guide to lead you step by step. Till now, you have completed five lessons. Up to here, things were easy, but now it will get complex as you move ahead. For that, it requires proper practice by writing the lesson from this book into your notebook and practicing the pronunciation of the words. If you ignore and do not do this, lessons from here will look difficult to you. So before moving ahead, make sure you have done proper practice till fifth lesson.

Just looking into this book with pleasure seeking attitude can make you laugh a little, as you see some words of German, but if you are really interested to learn, then be serious about it. Don't jump off and scroll down to the other pages without having proper practice done on all the previous lessons. Why it is necessary is that while learning a foreign language, even your single mistake will push your so much down, from where you can't even think of starting back again. If English is your first language, imagine how the other people learn it! I can tell you, English is also not easy to billions of people of the world. Many learn English after great efforts.

In the same way, you have to make efforts to learn this language. You won't learn it automatically, because if it was so easy, there was no need to buy this book. You would have learnt it by yourself. There are many people who want to learn a new language because it is very much fascinating, but many of them fail in the beginning only because they don't practice. For them, grapes are sour!

What is easy in the world? And if something is easy, what benefit the easy thing can give you? Nothing. If you want great success, you have to do great work. Remember that only difficult thing brings amazing success in your life. So refrain yourself from behaving like a play-boy learner and be a little serious about it – about German.

(1) You can enjoy the world of German only after you completely go through this book.
(2) Once you are thorough, you may need to buy a German-to-English dictionary.
(3) After this book, you may refer to my next book: **Foreign Languages Conversation**.
(4) Google Translate will help you a lot in learning while going through this book.
(5) If you get a chance to communicate with native German, it will be fabulous.

Wishing you all the best! Don't quit, continue learning.

Lesson 6
Some words

These are different kind of words of German language. Write them in your notebook and pronounce them correctly. You may have to try again and again as you might not pronounce them correctly in first attempt. Pronunciation is not a major concern in German, just you need to practice by seeing the pronunciation hint in the bracket or listening to it online.

Tee (tee) = tea
Zimmer (tseemer) = room
Haus (haws) = house
Sohn (zon) = son
Wahrheit (vaar-haa-it) = truth
mann (maan) = man
Held (helt) = hero

Teppich (tepish) = carpet
Regen (regen) = rain
Honig (honish) = honey
Sonntag (zontaak) = Sunday
Sommer (zomer) = summer
Brot (brot) = bread
Winter (winter) = winter

silbern (zilbern) = silver
Thron (tron) = throne
krank (kraank) = ill
schwer (shwer) = difficult [sh+v+ay+r]
Morgen (morgen) = morning
Abend (aabent) = evening
Name (naame) = name

Keksen (keksen) = Biscuits
Suppe (zoope) = soup
purpurn (purpurn) = purple
Woche (wokhe) = week
Zunge (tsunge) = tongue
Kinn (kin) = chin
Boden (boden) = floor

Exercise: -
Write the meaning of these words in German and pronounce them correctly.

Water, stove, when, mad
Word, difficult, morning, true
Evening, husband, lame, fruit

Lesson 7
Compound letters

The compound 'sch' is pronounced 'sh'.
fleisch (flaa-ish)   = flesh
schwager (shwaager)   = brother-in-law
schreiben (shraa-iben) = to write

The compound 'sp' sounds like 'shp'.
Spalt (shpaalt)   = crack
Spiegelei (shpeegelaai) = fried egg

If 'ch' comes after the letter a,o,u,au, then it is pronounced like 'kh' with <u>heavy throat sound</u>.
Bach (baakh)   = stream
hoch (hokh)   = high, tall
Kuchen (kookhen)   = cake
Rauch (rawkh)   = smoke ['aw' as it is pronounced in 'rock']
Tochter (tokhter)   = daughter

The letter 'ch' gives the sound of 'sh' when it comes after e, i, ö, ü, eu.
ich (ish)   = I
nicht (nisht)   = not
Bücher (byu-sher)   = books

The compound 'st' coming in the beginning of a word sounds like 'sht'.
Stuhl (Shtool)   = chair
stumm (shtoom)   = dumb

If 'st' appears in the middle of a word or after 'ch', then it sounds 'st'.
Fenster (fenster)   = window
nächste (ne-a-shte)   = next

The compound 'th' is pronounced as 't'.
Thron (tron)   = throne
Theater (te-aa-ter)   = theatre

The name of this new letter 'β' is (es-zet). It is an extra letter in German to be pronounced like 'ss'. It is used very less in German.
groβ (gross)   = big, long
Straβe (shtraa-sse)   = street

Lesson 8
Umlauts

The umlauts are placed on the three letters – a, o, u. After placing umlauts, they look like ä, ö, ü and their pronunciation gets modified.

The letter ä after umlaut has two sounds – long and short. The long sound is like (ei) as 'say' in English.
Käse (kei-ze)   = cheese

The short sound of this letter is (e) as 'set' in English.
Gepäck (gepek)   = luggage

The letter ö has no equivalent in English. It is pronounced like – Round 'U', after you round your lips.
schön (shun)   = beautiful
söhne (zune)   = sons
größer (gruser)   = bigger

The letter ü is pronounced like 'eu' as b**eau**ty in English.
müssen (myusen)   = must
grün (gryun)   = green [gre+u+n]
fünf (fyunf)   = five

These three letters 'ä, ö, ü' have long sound when they are followed by a consonant letter or if they come at the end of a word. Sometimes, they are pronounced short when they are followed by two or more consonants. But there are some exceptions to these rules also which will be getting clear to you as you move ahead. Don't worry, just keep moving.

Exercise: -
Write the meaning of these words in German and pronounce them correctly.
Beautiful, stream, morning, bigger
Sons, dumb, difficult, chair
Name, cake, fruit, tall
True, evening, five, water

Write the meaning of these words in English and pronounce them correctly.
Stuhl, Kuchen, krank, silbern
söhne, größer, stumm, Bach
schwer, hoch, Thron, Abend
Name, Käse, nächste, schwager

Lesson 9
Nouns and Articles
The name of a person, place or thing is called noun. All the nouns whether they are living or non-living, are categorized as masculine, feminine and <u>neuter</u> gender. You can find the gender of any noun by looking into a German dictionary. To distinguish the gender of a particular noun, the definite article 'the' is used. The article is used before noun and <u>undergoes</u> a change in accordance with the gender and number of the accompanying noun.

The father (mas)	= der Vater (der faater)
The mother (fem)	= die Mutter (dee mooter)
The money (neuter)	= das Geld (daas gelt)
The man	= der Mann (maan)
The woman	= die Frau (fraa-oo)
The ship	= das Schiff (shif)

From the above examples, you have noticed the three forms of definite articles 'the' as – der, die, das. These precede the noun depending on its gender and number. Here are a few more examples of nouns in all the three genders.

<u>Masculine Nouns</u>

der König (kunish)	= the king
der Student (shtoodent)	= the student
der Freund (froynt)	= the friend
der Lehrer (lerer)	= the teacher
der Apfel (aafel)	= the apple
der Brief (breef)	= the letter
der Bruder (brooder)	= the brother
der Bäcker (bei-ker)	= the baker

<u>Feminine Nouns</u>

die Konıgın (kuneegın)	= the queen
die Studentin (shtoodentin)	= the female student
die Freundin (froyndin)	= the female friend
die Lehrerin (lererin)	= the female teacher
die Schwester (shwester)	= the sister
die Tasse (taase)	= the cup
die Milch (milsh)	= the milk
die Schule (shoole)	= the school

<u>Neuter Nouns</u>

das Buch (bookh)	= the book
das Feld (felt)	= the field
das Auto (aa-u-to)	= the car
das Dach (daakh)	= the roof
das Vogel (fogel)	= the bird
das Boden (boden)	= the floor
das Hemd (hemt)	= the shirt
das Messer (meser)	= the knife

Lesson 10
Plural Nouns and Articles

The gender categorization in German is not based on any rule but it is a tradition that followed. Looking at the article of the word suggests you the gender. Otherwise, you need to look into a dictionary and find out the gender. And it is not a one-day task but takes a period of time to understand clearly.

As already said, the definite article undergoes a change according to the gender of the accompanying noun. Now we will see what happens with plural nouns. Please pay attention to it, otherwise, it may appear complicated to you.

<u>Plural Nouns</u>

The father	= der Vater (faater)
The fathers	= die Väter (feiter)
The mother	= die Mutter (mooter)
The mothers	= die Mütter (myuter)
The letter	= der Brief (breef)
The letters	= die Briefe (breefe)
The man	= der Mann (maan)
The men	= die Männer (mener)
The woman	= die Frau (fraau)
The women	= die frauen (fraau-en)
The roof	= das Dach (daakh)
The roofs	= die Dächer (deikher)

The first thing what we notice here is that in the <u>Plural of all the three genders – masculine, feminine and neuter </u>only the article 'die' is used. And one thing that may have surprised you is that in German – the <u>rule of changing singular into plural </u>is quite different from English. And it will be explained in the next lessons. So, the fathers = die Väter, (not die ~~Vaters~~). It is also necessary to mention here that – the <u>gender categorization </u>in German is quite different, and so:

The girl	= das Mädchen (mayt-shen)
The girls	= die Mädchen

The word 'girl' is a neuter noun in German because of its ending as –chen. Similarly, the word – the miss = das Fräulein (froilaain) is also neuter. But don't get afraid, you will be explained everything step by step. The only thing I will say here that the time when German was created, there was no logic to call it illogical.

Exercise: -
Write the meaning of these words in German.
The apple, the letter, the brother, the cup, the milk, the school, the bird, the floor, the book, the field, the car, the roof, the money, the fathers

Lesson 11
Singular - Plural

This lesson describes the rules of changing a singular noun into plural. This lesson requires a proper attention while learning.

Rule 1
<u>Masculine</u> or <u>neuter</u> nouns ending in –el, –en, –er do not undergo any change in the plural except taking umlaut on first vowel (exception applicable). Their plural is indicated by accompanying article only.

der Onkel (onkel)	= the uncle
die Onkel	= the uncles
der Apfel	= the apple
die Äpfel (eifel)	= the apples
der Garten (gaarten)	= the garden
die Gärten (gerten)	= the gardens
der Laden (laaden)	= the shop
die Läden (leden)	= the shops
der Bruder	= the brother
die Brüder (bryuder)	= the brothers
der Lehrer	= the teacher
die Lehrer	= the teachers
das Boden	= the floor (neuter)
die Böden (buden)	= the floors

Rule 2
Some masculine nouns, while chaning into plural, take 'e' at the end but <u>do not take</u> umlaut.

der Tag (taak)	= the day
die Tage (taage)	= the days
der Hund (hunt)	= the dog
die Hunde (hunde)	= the dogs
der Brief (breef)	= letter
die Briefe (breefe)	= letters

Rule 3
Some masculine nouns take both 'e' and <u>umlaut</u> to become plural.

der Gast (gaast)	= the guest
die Gäste (geste)	= the guests
der Tisch (tish)	= the table
die Tische (tishe)	= the tables

Rule 4
Some masculine nouns take 'er' at the end and umlaut to become plural.

der Wurm (wurm)	= the worm
die Würmer (wyurmer)	= the worms

der Mann (maan)	= man
die Männer (mener)	= men
das Kind (kint)	= the child
die Kinder (kinder)	= the children

Rule 5

The masculine or neuter nouns which do not end with –el, –en, –er, they take 'en' to become plural.

der Soldat (zoldaat)	= the soldier
die Soldaten	= the soldiers
der Bär (ber)	= the bear
die Bären (beren)	= the bears
das Bett (bet)	= the bed
die Betten	= the beds

Rule 6

The <u>feminine</u> singular nouns take –n or –en and umlaut to become plural.

die Tante (taante)	= the aunt
die Tanten (taanten)	= the aunts
die Dame (dame)	= the lady
die Damen	= the ladies
die Nacht (naakht)	= the night
die Nächte (neshte)	= the nights
die Magd (maagt)	= the maid
die Mägde (megde)	= the maids
die Wand (waant)	= the wall
die Wände (wende)	= the walls
die Hand (haant)	= the hand
die Hände (hende)	= the hands
die Schwester	= the sister
die Schwestern	= the sisters
die Tür (tyur)	= the door
die Türen (tyuren)	= the doors

It is said again that the singular-plural management may appear complicated to those who do not pay attention and practice by writing and speaking. This is one of the most important lessons of this book. German is similar to English but not exactly the same, so continue learning, and don't give up.

Exercise: -
Write the meaning of these words in German.
The bear, the bears, the wall, the walls, the night, the nights, the guest, the guests, the dog, the dogs, the floor, the floors, the apple, the apples

Lesson 12
Indefinite Article

As we use 'a' or 'an' indefinite article in English, so we use 'ein' (aa-in) for the masculine nouns and 'eine' (aa-i-ne) for the feminine nouns. We are emphasizing here the rule of indefinite article.

ein Mann	= a man
eine Frau	= a woman
ein Buch	= a book
eine Tasse	= a cup
ein Brief	= a letter
eine Schule	= a school
ein Apfel	= an apple
eine Hand	= a hand
ein Soldat	= a soldier
eine Nacht	= a night
ein kind	= a child [Neuter]
eine Tante	= an aunt
ein Haus	= a house
eine Königin	= a queen
ein Auge (aauge)	= an eye [Neuter]
ein ohr (or)	= an ear [Neuter]
ein Bett (bet)	= a bed [Neuter]
ein Ei (aai)	= an egg [Neuter]
ein Soldat	= a soldier
eine Dame	= a lady
ein Gast	= a guest
eine Schwester	= a sister

Exercise: -
Write the meaning of these words in German.

A man, a woman, the man, the woman, the men, the women, a brother, a sister, the brother, the sister, the brothers, the sisters, an uncle, an aunt, the uncle, the aunt, the uncles, the aunts, a father, a mother, the father, the mother, the fathers, the mothers

Lesson 13
Gender

As already said, there are three kinds of gender in German – masculine, feminine and neuter. Generally the nouns which end in **–e** are <u>feminine</u> and those which do not end in –e are masculine. So the ending of a word determines the gender.

Now, there are some rules to change the gender of a noun.
1. Some masculine words take '–in' at the end to become feminine.
Held (helt)   = hero
Heldin (heldin)   = heroine

König (kunish)   = king
Königin (kuneegin)   = queen

Spieler (shpeeler)   = player
Spielerin (shpeelerin)   = female player

2. Nouns ending in –ung, –keit, –ei, –schaft, –nis are feminine.
Zeitung (tsai-tung)   = newspaper
Freundschaft (froyent-shaaft) = friendship
Erlaubnis (erlaaupnis)   = permission

3. Most of the abstract nouns in German are feminine.
Wahrheit (waarhait)   = truth
Schönheit (shunhait)   = beauty
Sklaverei (sklaaveraai)   = slavery
Reinheit (raayenhait)   = purity

4. Most of the nouns with the prefix 'ge-' are neuter.
Gesicht (gezisht)   = face
Gebein (gebaain)   = bones
Gefäss (gefes)   = vessel

5. The nouns ending in –chen or –lein are neuter.
Kindlein (keendlaain)   = baby
Fräulein (froylaain)   = young lady
Kätzchen (ketshen)   = kitten

6. Most of the nouns ending in –en are masculine.
Garten (gaarten)   = garden
Regen (regen)   = rain
Kuchen (kookhen)   = cake

7. The two-syllable nouns ending in –ig, –ing, and –ich are masculine.
Liebling (leeplink)   = darling
Teppich (tepish)   = carpet
Honig (honish)   = honey

Lesson 14
Some Masculine – Feminine Words

Fürst (fyurst)	= prince
Fürstin (fyurstin)	= princess
Freund (froyent)	= male friend
Freundin (froyendin)	= female friend
Lehrer (lerer)	= male teacher
Lehrerin (lererin)	= female teacher
Bettler (betler)	= male beggar
Bettlerin (betlerin)	= female beggar
Schwager (shwaager)	= brother-in-law
Schwägerin (sheigerin)	= sister-in-law
Held (helt)	= hero
Heldin (heldin)	= heroine
Student (shtudent)	= male student
Studentin (shtudentin)	= female student
Ehemann (ehemaan)	= husband
Ehefrau (ehefraau)	= wife
Schwager-sohn (shwaager-zon)	= son-in-law
Schwager-tochter	= daughter-in-law
Neffe (nefe)	= nephew
Nichte (nishte)	= niece
Pferd (pfert)	= horse
Stute (shtoote)	= mare

Exercise: -
Write the meaning of these words in German.
Beauty, darling, truth, carpet, heroine, honey, female beggar, brother-in-law, purity, young lady, kitten, slavery

Write the meaning of these words in English.
Lehrer, Honig, Liebling, Teppich, Wahrheit, Schönheit, Sklaverei, Reinheit, Kindlein, Fräulein, Kätzchen, Held, Lehrerin, Bettler, Heldin, Schwager

Lesson 15
Forming Sentences with Adjective

Forming sentences with adjectives in German is different from English. In German, the adjectives change according to the gender, number and case of nouns. For example:

Rule 1: With Indefinite Article

Good   = gut (goot)

A good man (mas)	= ein guter Mann (gooter)
A good woman (fem)	= eine gute Frau (goote)
A good book (neuter)	= ein gutes Buch (gootes)

In these sentences the adjective 'gut' has declined as follows:
With a masculine singular noun > gut+er
With a feminine singular noun > gut+e
With a neuter singular noun > gut+es

Rule 2: With Definite Article

Good   = gut (goot)

The good man	= der gute Mann (goote)
The good woman	= die gute Frau
The good book	= das gute Buch
The good boys	= die guten Knaben (gooten)

<u>Other Examples</u>

Old wine (m)	= alter Wein (waa-in)
Old mother (f)	= alte Mutter
Old book (n)	= altes Buch
Red hat (m)	= roter Hut
Red ink (f)	= rote Tinte (tinte)
Red water (n)	= rotes Wasser (waaser)

Some Adjectives

warm (waarm)	= warm
kalt (kaalt)	= cold
neu (noy)	= new
alt (aalt)	= old
lieber (leeber)	= dear
großer (groser)	= large
bester (bester)	= best
runden (runden)	= round
groß (gros)	= tall
bedacht (bedaakht)	= careful
talentiert (taalenteert)	= talented
frisch (frish)	= fresh
rein (raayen)	= clean
schmutzig (shmoot-tsish)	= dirty

taub (taaup)	= deaf
dumm (dum)	= stupid
fleissig (flaay-sish)	= hardworking
faul (faaul)	= lazy
durstig (durstish)	= thirsty
hungrig (hungrish)	= hungry
breit (braayet)	= broad
hässlich (heslish)	= ugly
eng (eng)	= narrow
lustig (lustish)	= merry

One step ahead

little = klein (klaain)

A little daughter (f)	= eine kleine Tochter
The little daughter	= die kleine Tochter

sad = traurig (traaurish)

A sad girl (f)	= eine traurige Mädchen (traaurige)
The sad girl	= das traurige Mädchen

clever = klug (klook)

A clever boy (m)	= ein kluger Junge (kluger)
The clever boy	= der kluge Junge

pretty = hübsch (hyupsh)

A pretty girl (f)	= eine hübsche Mädchen
The pretty girl	= das hübsche Mädchen

short = kurz (kurts)

A short letter (m)	= ein kurzer Brief (kurtser)
The short letter	= der kurze Brief

clean = rein (raayen)

A clean handkerchief (n)	= ein reines Taschentuch (taashentukh)
The clean handkerchief	= das reine Taschentuch

new = neu (noy)

A new dress (n)	= ein neues Kleid (klaa-it)
The new dress	= das neue Kleid

old = alt (aalt)

An old castle (n)	= ein altes Schloß (shlos)
The old castle	= das alte Schloß

Exercise: -
Translate these sentences into German.
A tall man, the tall man, a tall woman, the tall woman, a new boy, the new boy, a new girl, the new girl,
a talented son, the talented son, a talented daughter, the talented daughter

Lesson 16
Comparisons

The comparative of adjective is always formed by adding –er to the positive degree, and –st, –ste in the superlative degree.

small	= klein (klaa-in) [positive]
smaller	= kleiner (klaainer) [comparative]
smallest	= kleinst (klaainst) [superlative]
poor	= arm (aarm)
poorer	= ärmer (eirmer)
poorest	= ärmste (eirmste)
old	= alt (aalt)
older	= älter (eilter)
oldest	= älteste (eilteste)
big	= gross
bigger	= grosser (gruser)
biggest	= grösste (gruste)

The adjective ending in –d, –t, –s, –ss, –sch, –z or vowel takes 'st' in superlative. And the adjective ending in –el, –er, –en, –m takes 'ste'. Many adjectives take umlaut in comparison and many do not.

hard	= hart (haart)
harder	= härter
hardest	= härtest
noble	= edel (edel)
nobler	= edler
noblest	= edelste
stupid	= dumm (dum)
stupider	= dümmer (dyumer)
stupidest	= dümmste (dyumste)
full	= voll (fol)
fuller	= voller
fullest	= vollst
happy	= froh (fro)
happier	= froher
happiest	= frohest
brave	= tapfer (taap-fer)
braver	= tapferer
bravest	= tapferste

Lesson 17
Case

The case has a different set of rules which affects the indefinite and definite articles of the nouns. Write these examples in your notebook and frame some sentences of your own to make sure you understand the rule of case. The case will be explained in lesson 30.

<u>Objective Case</u>
A man (m)   = ein Mann
A woman (f)   = eine Frau
A book (n)   = ein Buch

<u>Genitive Case</u>
of a man   = eines Mann (aaynes)
of a woman   = einer Frau (aayner)
of a book   = eines Buch (aaynes)

<u>Dative Case</u>
to / for a man   = einem Mann (aaynem)
to / for a woman   = einer Frau
to / for a book   = einem Buch

<u>Definite Article Case</u>
the father   = der Vater
of the father   = des Vaters*
to / for the father   = dem Vater
of the house   = des Hauses

*For the meaning 'of', in masculine and neuter nouns, the letter '–s' is added at the end of a noun. For example: Julias = of Julia / Julia's, Manns = of man / man's.

Exercise: -
Translate these sentences into German.
A man, the man, of a man, of the man, to a man, to the man, the men, of the men, to the men, a woman, the woman, of a woman, of the woman, to a woman, to the woman, the women, of the women, to the women

Translate these sentences into German.
The brave father, the happiest man, the noblest woman, the big book, the oldest letter, the poorest student, the small school, the happy mother, the big house, a little daughter, the sad girl, the clever boy, a pretty girl, a short letter, the new dress, the old castle

Lesson 18
Days and Moths

The name of days, months and seasons are all masculine in German, so the article 'der' should be used with all.

Monday	= der Montag (montaak)
Tuesday	= der Dienstag (deenstaak)
Wednesday	= der Mittwoch (mitvokh)
Thursday	= der Donnerstag (donerstaak)
Friday	= der Freitag (fraaytaak)
Saturday	= der Samstag (zaamstaak)
Sunday	= der Sonntag (zontaak)

January	= der Januar (yaanu-aar)
February	= der Februar (febru-aar)
March	= der März (meirts)
April	= der April (aapril)
May	= der Mai (maa-i)
June	= der Juni (yooni)
July	= der Juli (yooli)
August	= der August (aaugust)
September	= der September (zeptember)
October	= der Oktober (oktober)
November	= der November (november)
December	= der Dezember (detsember)

Spring	= der Frühling (fryuling)
Summer	= der Sommer (zomer)
Autumn	= der Herbst (herpst)
Winter	= der Winter (winter)

The week	= die Woche (wokhe)
Next Monday	= nächsten Montag (neishten)
On Tuesday	= dem Dienstag
Last Wednesday	= letzten Mittwoch (letsten)
The weather	= das Wetter (weter)
The year	= das Jahr (yaar)

<u>Colors</u>

White	= weiss (vaa-is)
Black	= schwarz (shwaarts)
Brown	= braun
Yellow	= gelb (gaylp)
Green	= Grün (griyun)
Red	= rot
Pink	= rosa (rozaa)

Lesson 19
Numbers

One	= eins (aa-ins)
Two	= zwei (tswaay)
Three	= drei (draay)
Four	= vier (feer)
Five	= fünf (fyunf)
Six	= sechs (zeks)
Seven	= sieben (zeeben)
Eight	= acht (aakht)
Nine	= neun (noyen)
Ten	= zehn (tsen)
Eleven	= elf (elf)
Twelve	= zwölf (tso-elf)
Thirteen	= dreizehn (draaye-tsen)
Fourteen	= vierzehn (feer-tsen)
Fifteen	= fünfzehn (fyunf-tsen)
Sixteen	= sechzehn (zesh-tsen)
Seventeen	= siebzehn (zeep-tsen)
Eighteen	= achtzehn (aakh-tsen)
Nineteen	= neunzehn (noyen-tsen)
Twenty	= zwanzig (tswaan-tsish)

From twenty-one onwards the word 'und' is used in between. und = and

Twenty-one	= einundzwanzig (aai-unts-vaan-tsish) [ein+und+zwanzig]
Twenty-two	= zweiundzwanzig (tsvei-unts-vaan-tsish) [zwei+und+zwanzig]
Thirty	= dreißig (draaisish)
Forty	= vierzig (feer-tsish)
Fifty	= fünfzig (fyunf-tsish)
Sixty	= sechzig (zesh-tsish)
Seventy	= siebzig (zeep-tsish)
Eighty	= achtzig (aakh-tsish)
Ninety	= neunzig (noyen-tsish)
Hundred	= hundert (hundert)
One thousand	= ein tausend (taauzent)
One million	= eine Million (milee-on)

First	= erste (erste)
Second	= zweite (tswaayte)
Third	= dritte (drite)
Fourth	= vierte (feerte)
Fifth	= fünfte (fyunfte)
Sixth	= sechste (zekste)
Seventh	= siebte (zeepte)
Eighth	= achte (aakhte)
Ninth	= neunte (noyente)
Tenth	= zehnte (tsente)

Lesson 20
Parts of Body

The parts of body are also categorized as masculine, feminine or neuter gender. So the article der, die, or das has to be used with them. Though it is not necessary now, but later, you can look into your dictionary to find out the gender of a word.

Body	= Körper (kurper)
Face	= Gesicht (gezisht)
Head	= Kopf (kopf)
Eye	= Auge (aauge)
Ear	= Ohr (or)
Mouth	= Mund (munt)
Nose	= Nase (naaze)
Hand	= Hand (haant)
Finger	= Finger (finger)
Thumb	= Daumen (daaumen)
Arm	= Arm
Leg	= Bein (baa-in)
Neck	= Hals (haals)
Chest	= Brust (brust)
Foot	= Fuss (foos)
Chin	= Kinn (kin)
Cheek	= Backe (baake)
Lip	= Lippe (lipe)
Tongue	= Zunge (tsunge)
Stomach	= Magen (maagen)
Tooth	= Zahn (tsaan)
Elbow	= Ellbogen (elbogen)
Heel	= Hacke (haake)
Shoulder	= Schulter (shulter)
Palm	= Palme (paalme)
Nerves	= Nerven (nerfen)
Thigh	= Schenkel (shenkel)
Lung	= Lunge (lunge)
Liver	= Leber (leber)
Toe	= Zehe (tse-he)

Lesson 21
Relations

Parents	= Eltern (eltern)
Father	= Vater (faater)
Mother	= Mutter (mooter)
Brother	= Bruder (brooder)
Sister	= Schwester (shwester)
Uncle	= Onkel (onkel)
Aunt	= Tante (taante)
Cousin Brother	= Vetter (feter)
Cousin Sister	= Kusine (kuzeene)
Son	= Sohn (zon)
Daughter	= Tochter (tokhter)
Husband	= Ehemann (ehemaan)
Wife	= Ehefrau (ehefraau)
Nephew	= Neffe (nefe)
Niece	= Nichte (nishte)
Grandparent	= Grosseltern (groseltern)
Grandson	= Enkel (enkel)
Granddaughter	= Enkelin (enkelin)
Grandmother	= Grossmutter
Grandfather	= Grossvater
Brother-in-law	= Schwager (shwaager)
Sister-in-law	= Schwägerin (shweigerin)
Father-in-law	= Schwieger-vater (shweeger)
Mother-in-law	= Schwieger-mutter
Son-in-law	= Schwieger-sohn
Daughter-in-law	= Schwieger-tochter
Male Friend	= Freund (froyent)
Female Friend	= Freundin (froyendin)
Fiancé	= Bräutigam (broytigaam)
Fiancée	= Braut (braaut)
Lady	= Dame (daame)
Gentleman	= Herr (her)
Mr.	= Herr
Miss	= Fräulein (froylin)
Mrs.	= Frau
Unmarried	= Ledig (laydish)
Married	= Verheiratet (ferhaay-raatet)

Lesson 22
Eatables

Coffee	= Kaffee (kaafee)
Fruit	= Obst (opst)
Fish	= Fisch (fish)
Egg	= Ei (aa-i)
Flour	= Mehl (mel)
Butter	= Butter (buter)
Cream	= Sahne (zaane)
Wine	= Wein (waa-in)
Pastry	= Gebäck (gebek)
Ice	= Eis (aa-is)

Cutlet	= Schnitzel (shnitsel)
Lemonade	= Limonade (limonaade)
Apple	= Apfel (aafel)
Cherry	= Kirsche (kirshe)
Grapes	= Weintrauben (waa-in-traau-ben)
Banana	= Banane (banaane)
Lemon	= Zitrone (tsitrone)
Orange	= Apfelsine (aafelzine)
Jam	= Marmelade (maarmelaade)
Snack	= Imbiss

Noodles	= Nudeln (noodeln)
Onion	= Zwiebel (tsvaai-bel)
Potatoes	= Kartoffeln (kaartofeln)
Vegetable	= Gemüse (gemyuze)
Salt	= Salz (zaalts)
Soup	= Suppe (zupe)
Chicken	= Huhn (hoon)
Biscuits	= Keksen
Mutton	= Hammelfleish (haamel-flaa-ish)
Tomato	= Tomate (tomaate)
Salad	= Salat (zalaat)
Breakfast	= Frühstück (friyush-tyuk)
Lunch	= Mittagessen (mitaakesen)
Supper	= Abendbrot (aabentbrot)

Exercise: -
Write the meaning of these words in German.
Winter, tomato, orange, nephew, thumb, mouth, nose, biscuits, mutton, summer, July, niece, snack, son, eye, ear, April, head

Write the meaning of these words in English.
Frühling, Sommer, Herbst, Juni, Nase, Schenkel, Lunge, Leber, Zehe, Sohn, Tochter, Ehemann, Ehefrau, Neffe, Nichte, Zitrone, Apfelsine, Mermelade, Imbis, Huhn, Keksen, Hammelfleish

Lesson 23
Prepositions

On	= auf (aa-uf)
For	= für (fyur)
Without	= ohne (ohne)
Through	= durch (dursh)
Against	= gegen
About	= um (um)
After	= nach (naakh)
From	= von (fon)
In / into	= in
Of	= von
With	= mit
To	= zu (tsoo)
In front of	= vor (for)
Behind	= hinter
Near	= bei (baa-i)
Since	= seit (zaa-it)
At	= an (aan)
Because of	= wegen
Under	= unter (unter)
During	= während (weirent)

Pronouns

I	= ich (ish)
We	= wir (veer)
He	= er (er)
She	= sie (zee)
It	= es (es)
You	= Sie (zee) [Capital 'S']
They	= sie (zee)
Thou	= du (doo)
This	= dies (dees)
That	= das (daas)
These	= dies
Those	= das

The word 'sie' represents three pronouns. The 'Sie' meaning 'you' is written with capital 'S'. To resolve the doubt as to which of the other two sie means what we have to look at the accompanying verbs which will be explained in next lessons.

Lesson 24
Possessive Pronoun

```
My              = mein (maa-in) [mas & neuter]
                  meine (maa-ine) [fem & plural]


My uncle        = mein Onkel
My sister       = meine Schwester
My sisters      = meine Schwestern
My uncles       = meine Onkel
My pen          = meine Feder (feder) / mein Stiff (shtift)



Our             = unser (unzer) [mas & neuter]
                  unsere (unzere) [fem & plural]
Our uncle       = unser Onkel
Our sister      = unsere Schwester
Our sisters     = unsere Schwestern
Our uncles      = unsere Onkel
Our pen         = unsere Feder



His             = sein (zaayen) [mas & neuter]
                  seine (zaayne) [fem & plural]
His uncle       = sein Onkel
His sister      = seine Schwester
His sisters     = seine Schwestern
His uncles      = seine Onkel
His pen         = seine Feder



Your            = ihr (eer) [mas & neuter]
                  ihre (eere) [fem & plural]
Your uncle      = ihr Onkel
Your sister     = ihre Schwester
Your sisters    = ihre Schwestern
Your uncles     = ihre Onkel
Your pen        = ihre Feder



Their / her / its = ihr (eer) [mas & neuter]
                    ihre (eere) [fem & plural]
Their house     = ihr Häuser
Her mother      = ihre Mutter
Her nieces      = ihre Nichten
Their nieces    = ihre Nichten
```

Lesson 25
Possessive Pronoun 'thy'

Thy	= dein (daayen) [mas & neuter]
	deine (daayne) [fem & plural]
Thy uncle	= dein Onkel
Thy sister	= deine Schwester
Thy sisters	= deine Schwestern
Thy uncles	= deine Onkel
Thy pen	= deine Feder

Objective Pronoun

Me / to me	= mir (meer)
Us / to us	= uns (uns)
Him / to him	= ihm (eem)
Her / to her	= ihr (eer)
You / to you	= ihnen (ihnen)
Them / to them	= sie (zee)
Thee	= dich (dish)

Interrogative Pronouns

Who	= wer (wer)
What	= was (was)
Where	= wo (wo)
Whom	= wen (wen)
Whose	= wessen (wesen)
Which	= welcher (welsher)
When	= wann (waan) / wenn (wen)
How	= wie (wee)
Why	= warum (waroom)

This is my uncle	= Das / dies ist mein Onkel. [ist = is]
Is this my uncle?	= Ist das mein Onkel?
That is our friend	= Das ist unsere Freund.
These are my books	= Dies sind meine Bücher. [sind = are]
Are these his books?	= Sind dies seine Bücher?
Those are good books	= Das sind gute Bücher.
I am in this class	= Ich bin in dieser Klasse. [bin = am]
Our house is in the street	= Unser Haus ist in der Straße.
She is tall	= Sie ist gross.
Where is the water?	= Wo ist das Wasser?
I am an Indian	= Ich bin ein Inder. (eender)
What is your father?	= Was ist ihr /dein Vater?

Note: - The usage of ist, sind, bin and other helping verbs are explained in the next lesson. This lesson was to introduce all the pronouns.

Lesson 26
Present Indefinite Tense

<u>Affirmative</u>
sein   = to be (zaa-in)

I am	= ich bin (ish bin)
We are	= wir sind (weer zint)
You are	= Sie sind (see zint)
They are	= sie sind (zee zint)
He is	= er ist (er ist)
She is	= sie ist (zee ist)
It is	= es ist (es ist)
Thou are	= du bist (doo bist)

The word 'sie' is used for you, she, they all the three pronouns. For you, 'Sie' begins with capital letter in writing. In familiar term, 'du' is used quite frequently for 'you' to avoid ambiguity. For other two pronouns, the meaning can be understood by seeing the verb form.

He is a man	= Er ist ein Mann.
I am a teacher	= Ich bin eine Lehrerin. (f)
You are beautiful	= Sie sind schön.
We are sisters	= Wir sind schwestern.
This is here	= Es / das ist hier.
This is night	= Es /das ist nacht.
I am thirsty	= Ich bin durstig.
We are girls	= Wir sind Mädchen.
They are there	= Sie sind dort.
We are wrong	= Wir sind falsch. (faalsh)
The apples are green	= Die Äpfel sind grün.

<u>Negative and Interrogative</u>

I am not	= ich bin nicht.
Am I not?	= bin ich nicht?
We are not	= wir sind nicht.
Are we not?	= sind wir nicht?
You are not	= Sie sind nicht.
Are you not?	= sind Sie nicht?
He is not	= er ist nicht.
Is he not?	= ist er nicht?
She is not	= sie ist nicht.
Is she not?	= ist sie nicht?

They are not	= sie sind nicht.
Are they not?	= sind sie nicht?

It is not	= es ist nicht.
Is it not?	= ist es nicht?

We are not there	= Wir sind nicht dort.
This is not a book	= Das ist nicht ein Buch.
I am not a student	= Ich bin nicht ein Student.
You are not a king	= Sie sind (du bist) nicht ein König.
She is not angry	= Sie ist nicht böse. (buze)

Are you hungry?	= Sind Sie (bist du) hungrig?
Is he not thirsty?	= Ist er nicht durstig?
Am I tall?	= Bin ich groß?
Are we not fat?	= Sind wir nicht dick?
Is it not false?	= Ist es nicht falsch?
Is she not thin?	= Ist sie nicht dünn?
It is not here not there	= Es ist nicht hier nicht dort.

The brother is poor	= Der Bruder ist arm.
Is the night not dark?	= Ist die nacht nicht dunkel?
She is not very tall	= Sie ist nicht sehr groß. (zer)
Is the nut ripe?	= Ist die Nuss reif? (noos, raa-if)
The tailor is bad	= Der Schneider ist schlecht. (shnaai-der, shlesht)
The maid is pretty	= Die Magd ist nett. (maagt, net)

Exercise: -
Translate these sentences into German.

I am a soldier. We are guests. You are a hero. They are teachers. He is a prince. She is a queen. It is a pen. We are brave. They are not poor. Is she old? Is it not big? That is here. We are brothers. I am hungry. We are students. Are you tall? Are we fat? Is he not thin? The man is a soldier. We are here. I am not a king.

Translate these sentences into English.

er ist ein Mann. ich bin eine Lehrerin. Sie sind schön. dies ist mein Onkel. ist dies mein Onkel? das ist unsere Freund. dies sind mein Bücher. sind dies sein Bücher? das sind gute Bücher. ich bin in dieser Klasse. wo ist das Wasser? es ist nicht ein Buch. ich bin nicht ein Student. Sie sind nicht ein König. sie ist nicht böse. sind Sie hungrig? ich bin ein Inder. was ist ihr Vater?

Lesson 27
Verbs in Present Indefinite

lieben (leeben) = to love
This verb has two parts – the stem (root), and the termination. 'lieb' is the stem which remains unchanged with any pronoun. But '-en' is the termination which undergoes changes with pronouns.

<u>Affirmative</u>
ich liebe (leebe)   = I love
wir lieben (leeben)   = we love
Sie lieben   = you love
sie lieben   = they love
er/sie/es liebt (leebt)   = he/she/it loves
du liebst (leebst)   = thou love [singular]
ihr liebt (eer)   = thou people love [plural]

In case of pronoun 'ich' – (I), the letter 'e' is added to the stem of the verb.
In 'Sie/wir/sie'– (you, we, they), the letter 'en' is added to the stem.
In 'er/sie/es/ihr'– (he/she/it/thou people), the letter 't' is added to the stem.
In 'du' – (thou), the letter 'st' is added to the stem.

<u>Negative</u>
ich liebe nicht   = I do not love.
wir lieben nicht   = we do not love.
Sie lieben nicht   = you do not love
sie lieben nicht   = they do not love
er/sie/es liebt nicht   = he/she/it does not love
du liebst nicht   = thou do not love
ihr liebt nicht   = thou people do not love

The rule of negative sentence is that the word 'nicht' comes after verb in German. But in English 'not' comes before verb.

<u>Interrogative</u>
liebe ich?   = Do I love?
lieben wir?   = Do we love?
lieben Sie?   = Do you love?
lieben sie?   = Do they love?

<u>Interrogative Negative</u>
liebe ich nicht?   = Do I not love?
lieben wir nicht?   = Do we not love?
lieben Sie nicht?   = Do you not love?
liebt sie nicht?   = Does she not love?

Lesson 28
Some verb forms

haben (haaben) = to have
ich habe   = I have
Sie/wir/sie haben   = you/we/they have
er/sie/es hat   = he/she/it has
du hast   = thou have

spielen (shpeelen) = to play
ich spiele   = I play
Sie/wir/sie spielen   = you/we/they play
er/sie/es spielt   = he/she/it plays
du spielst   = thou play

rauchen (raaukhen) = to smoke
ich rauche   = I smoke
Sie/wir/sie rauchen   = you/we/they smoke
er/sie/es raucht   = he/she/it smokes
du rauchst   = thou smoke

fragen (fraagen) = to ask
ich frage   = I ask
Sie/wir/sie fragen   = you/we/they ask
er/sie/es fragt   = he/she/it asks
du fragst   = thou ask

sehen (zehen) = to see
ich sehe   = I see
Sie/wir/sie sehen   = you/we/they see
er/sie/es sieht   = he/she/it sees (irregular verb form)
du siehst   = thou see

hören (huren) = to hear
ich höre   = I hear
Sie/wir/sie hören   = you/we/they hear
er/sie/es hört   = he/she/it hears
du hörst   = thou hear

wollen (wolen) = to want
ich will   = I want
Sie/wir/sie wollen   = you/we/they want
er/sie/es will   = he/she/it wants
du willst   = thou want

Lesson 29
Some verbs

kaufen (kaaufen)	= to buy
verkaufen (ferkaaufen)	= to sell
bringen (bringen)	= to bring
besuchen (bezookhen)	= to visit
empfangen (empfaangen)	= to receive [n = half 'n' sound]
wollen (wolen)	= to want
sehen (zehen)	= to see
loben	= to praise
kämpfen (keimpfen)	= fight
zugeben (tsoogeben)	= to admit
hören (huren)	= to hear
träumen (troi-men)	= to dream
wohnen	= to live
gehen (gehen)	= to go
warten	= to wait
antworten	= answer
arbeiten	= to work
mögen (mugen)	= to like

If the stem of a verb ends in d, t, m, n, then before using terminator –t or –st, the letter 'e' is placed in the middle to make the pronunciation easy. The same rule is applied if a stem ends in the letter s, z, ss.

du atmest	= thou breathe
du tanzest	= thou dance
du reisest (raai-zest)	= thou travel
du öffnest	= thou open

Present Continuous Tense
There is no Present Continuous Tense in German. Instead of that Present Indefinite tense is used.

I play/I am playing	= ich spiele.
She does not play/She is not playing	= sie spielt nicht?
Do you ask/Are you asking?	= fragen Sie?
Do I not sell/Am I not selling?	= verkaufe ich nicht?
Do they not visit/Are they not visiting?	= besuchen sie nicht?
Do I see/Am I seeing?	= sehe ich?
Thou travel/Thou are travelling	= du reisest
He smokes/he is smoking	= er raucht

Exercise: -
Translate these sentences into German.
I play. I do not play. Do I play? Do I not play? We play. We do not play. Do we play? Do we not play? She plays. She does not play. Does she play? Does she not play? Thou play. Thou do not play. Do thou play? Do thou not play?   I go. I do not go. Do I go? Do I not go? We go. We do not go. Do we go? Do we not go? She goes. She does not go. Does she go? Does she not go? Thou go. Thou do not go. Do thou go? Do thou not go?

Lesson 30
Accusative Case

Case indicates the role of a noun in a sentence. **Nominative Case**: Subject performs the action. **Accusative Case**: Subject directly receives the action. **Dative Case**: Subject indirectly receives the action. **Genetive Case**: Subject serves as owner of relative. In Accusative Case, an object of the sentence is accused of an incident. In this case, the object takes the definite article 'den' instead of der, die or das. And for indefinite article, it takes 'einen' instead of ein. The accusation of this case is similar to emphasis of English when you put stress on something while saying.

The sentences in Accusative Case

He has <u>a</u> dog	= Er hat <u>einen</u> Hund. [Using 'a' you emphasize dog]
Do you have <u>the</u> book?	= Haben Sie <u>den</u> Buch? [Using 'the' you emphasize book]
Who has <u>the</u> letter?	= Wer hat <u>den</u> Brief? [Emphasizing 'the']
Do you have <u>an</u> umbrella?	= Haben Sie <u>einen</u> Schirm? (sheerm)
I have <u>an</u> uncle	= Ich habe <u>einen</u> Onkel.

Does she have an apple?	= Hat sie ein Apfel? [No emphasis – no Accusative]
Do they not have the car?	= Haben sie das Auto nicht? [No emphasis] [Object shifts before]
He has money	= Er hat das Geld. [No emphasis]
We have books.	= Wir haben die Bücher. [No emphasis]

Present Perfect Tense
In this tense, the regular verbs take 'ge-' before the stem and take '-t' at the place of termination. That means: 'ge–' prefix and '–t' termination. For example: -

I have bought.
For this – I have = ich habe
Now for 'bought' – ge+kauf+t

I have bought	= ich habe gekauft.

Once again it is said that to make a past participle of a verb, you have to add 'ge-' before the stem and just '-t' as termination.

You have bought	= Sie haben gekauft.
We have asked	= Wir haben gefragt.
I have heard	= Ich habe gehört.
They have waited	= Sie haben gewartet.
He has answered	= Er hat geantwortet.
She has worked	= Sie hat gearbeitet.
Thou have loved	= Du hast geliebt.
Thou people have heard	= Ihr habt gehört.

Exercise: -
Translate these sentences into German.

I play. I do not play. Do I play? I am playing. I am not playing. Am I playing? I have played. He plays. He does not play. Does he play? He is playing. He is not playing. Is he playing? He has played.

Lesson 31
Step-ahead for Present Perfect

Irregular Verbs
Till now, the verbs that you learnt were regular verbs, and so, they had a fix rule to change their termination. But there are some irregular verbs also which do not have a fixed rule while changing into past participle form.

These irregular verbs take '-ge' as a prefix, but the vowels in the verbs undergo some changes.
do   = tun
done   = getan
drink   = trinken
drunk   = getrunken
speak   = sprechen (shpreshen)
spoken   = gesprochen
play   = spielen
played   = gespielt

Some verbs which end in 'ieren', do not take '-ge' as prefix. And some other verbs which start with 'be' also do not take '-ge' as prefix.
study   = studieren
studied   = studiert
visit   = besuchen
visited   = besucht

Negative of Present Perfect
I have not visited   = Ich habe nicht besucht.
They have not come   = Sie haben nicht gekommen.
He has not spoken   = Er hat nicht gesprochen.
She has not asked   = Sie hat nicht gefragt.
You have not heard   = Du hast (Sie haben) nicht gehört.
We have not begun   = Wir haben nicht begonnen.
You have not eaten   = Du hast (Sie haben) nicht gegessen.

Interrogative of Present Perfect
Have I visited?   = Habe ich besucht?
Have they not come?   = Haben sie nicht gekommen?
Have they drunk?   = Haben sie getrunken?
Has he understood?   = Hat er verstanden?
Have you sold this?   = Hast du (haben Sie) das verkauft? [Object before main verb]
Has she not received?   = Hat sie nicht gefunden?

Exercise: -
Translate these sentences into German.

He has worked. He has not worked. Has he worked? Has he not worked? We have sold. We have not sold. Have we sold? Have we not sold? You have heard this. You have not heard this. Have you heard this? Have you not heard this?

Lesson 32
Step-ahead for Present Perfect
There are some verbs which do not agree with 'haben' but they agree with 'sien = to be' for present perfect tense. The verbs are: -

gegangen	= gone
gekommen	= come
geblieben	= stayed

I am	= ich bin
I have (am) come	= ich bin gekommen
He has (is) gone	= er ist gegangen
She has (is) stayed	= sie ist geblieben

been	= gewesen
I have (am) been	= Ich bin gewesen.
We have (are) not been out	= wir sind nicht aus gewesen. [Participle comes at the end]
Have you not been there?	= Sind Sie nicht dort gewesen?
They have been here	= Sie sind hier gewesen.
Who has been there?	= Wer ist dort gewesen?

<u>Some past participle</u>

studied	= studiert (shtudi-ert)
answered	= geantwortet
visited	= besucht (bezukht)
finished	= geendet (ge-endet)
done	= gearbeitet
opened	= geöffnet
put / had (v3)	= gehabt

I have played	= Ich habe gespielt.
I have studied	= Ich habe studiert.
You have answered	= Sie haben geantwortet.
We have visited	= Wir haben besucht.
I have finished	= Ich habe geendet.
They have done	= Sie haben gearbeitet.
He has answered	= Er hat geantwortet.
She has opened	= Sie hat geöffnet.
Thou have put / had	= Du hast gehabt.

Note: - There is no Present Perfect Continuous tense. Present Perfect tense is same to **Past Indicative** tense. Past Indicative is the part of Past Indefinite tense which shows an action done just one time.

Exercise: - Translate these sentences into German.
You play. You do not play. Do you play? Do you not play? You are playing. You are not playing. Are you playing? Are you not playing? You have played. You have not played. Have you played? Have you not played? You have been playing. You have not been playing. Have you been playing? Have you not been playing?

Lesson 33
Past Indefinite (Past Historic) Tense

I/he/she/it was	= ich/er/sie/es war.
You/we/they were	= Sie/wir/sie warren.
Thou were	= du warst.
You people were	= ihr wart.

With I, he, she, it and singular noun, the verb drops its final '-en' and adds '-te' to the stem. With you, we, they and plural noun, the verb drops '-en' and adds '-ten' to the stem.

love – lieben
I/he/she/it loved	= ich/er/sie/es liebte.
You/we/they loved	= Sie/wir/sie liebten.
Thou loved	= du liebtest.
You people loved	= ihr liebtet.

say – sagen
ich/er/sie/es sagte
Sie/wir/sie sagten
du sagtest
ihr sagtet

play – spielen
ich/er/sie/es spielte
Sie/wir/sie spielten
du spieltest
ihr spieltet

They smoked	= sie rauchten.
We visited	= wir besuchten.
They did not smoke	= sie rauchten nicht.
We did not visit	= wir besuchten nicht.
Did they smoke?	= rauchten sie?
Did we visit?	= besuchten wir?

We sat	= wir setzten.
He did not ask	= er fragte nicht.
They did not sell	= sie verkauften nicht.
You did not buy	= Sie kauften nicht.
Did you not hear?	= hörten Sie nicht?
Did they not sell?	= verkauften sie nicht?
Did I not come?	= Kam ich nicht?
Did I not ask?	= Fragte ich nicht?

<u>Some sentences with irregular verbs</u>

I knew him	= Ich kannte ihm.
He bought this	= Er kaufte es.
They began	= Sie begannen
Why did they not speak?	= Warum sprachen sie nicht? (shprakhen)
He gave me a book	= Er gab mir ein Buch.
We did not help them	= Wir halfen ihnen nicht.
We went	= Wir gingen.
I came	= Ich kam.
He did	= er tat.
He went to house	= er ging nach Hause. [nach = to]

Because these are irregular verbs, so you may face some problem while understanding these sentences. But don't worry; as you move ahead, things would get clearer to you.

<u>Verbs in Past Indefinite form</u>

send	= senden
sent	= sandte
run	= rennen
ran	= rannte
burn	= brennen
burnt	= brannte
love	= lieben
loved	= liebte
say	= sagen
said	= sagte
play	= spielen
played	= spielte
think	= denken
thought	= dachte
bring	= bringen
brought	= brachte

* The reason to give more focus to this tense is that again there is no Past Continuous tense ahead. Instead of Past Continuous, Past Indefinite tense is used.
* Past Indefinite has two tenses – 1. Past Indicative (as onetimer), 2. Past Historic (as multi-timer – also equal to 'Past Continuous and 'Used to').
* Generally, only three tenses – 1. **Present Indefinite**, 2. **Present Perfect** (also as Past Indicative), 3. **Future Indefinite** is used much in German.

Shifting and Reshifting

'nicht' in negative sentence with / without object

I do not play	= Ich spiele nicht.
I do not play cricket	= Ich spiele kein Cricket. (kein = no)
I have not played	= Ich habe nicht gespielt.
I have not played cricket	= Ich habe kein Cricket gespielt.
I have played cricket	= Ich habe Cricket gespielt.

Lesson 34
Past Perfect Tense
To form sentences in Past Perfect, we have to use 'hatte' (haatay), which is applied as (had) of English. After this, past participle form is used which you have already learnt. Following is the list of 'hatte' changing with pronouns.

had – hatte
I/he/she/it had	= ich/er/sie/es hatte.
You/we/they had	= Sie/wir/sie hatten.
Thou had	= du hattest.
You people had	= ihr hattet.

I had played	= ich hatte gespielt.
I had studied	= ich hatte studiert.
You had answered	= Sie hatten geantwortet.
We had visited	= wir hatten besucht.
I had finished	= ich hatte geendet.
They had done	= sie hatten gearbeitet.
He had answered	= er hatte geantwortet.
She had opened	= sie hatte geöffnet.
Thou had put	= du hattest gehabt.
They had waited	= sie hatten gewartet.
Thou had bought	= du hattest gekauft.
She had opened	= sie hatte geöffnet.
I had become	= ich hatte geworden.
He had had	= er hatte gehabt.
I had (was) been	= ich war gewesen.

Negative and Interrogative
I had not played	= ich hatte nicht gespielt.
I had not studied	= ich hatte nicht studiert.
Had I played?	= hatte ich gespielt?
Had I studied?	= hatte ich studiert?
Had I not played?	= hatte ich nicht gespielt?
Had I not studied?	= hatte ich nicht studiert?

We had not waited	= wir hatten nicht gewartet.
I had not answred	= ich hatte nicht geantwortet.
Had he waited?	= hatte er gewartet?
I had not become	= ich hatte nicht geworden.
Had she not answred?	= hatte sie nicht geantwortet?
Had you waited?	= hatten Sie gewartet?
Had she written?	= hatte sie geschrieben? (geshreeben)

Exercise: -
Translate these sentences into German.
We have studied. We have not studied. Have we studied? Have we not studied? We had studied. We had not studied. Had we studied? Had we not studied?

Lesson 35
Future Indefinite Tense
To form sentences in Future Indefinite, we have to use 'werde (vayrday)', which is applied as (shall/will) word of English. After this, the complete verb is used without dropping termination. Following is the list of 'werde' changing with pronouns.

shall/will – werde (werde)

I shall	= ich werde.
He/she/it will	= er/sie/es wird.
You/we/they will	= Sie/wir/sie werden.
Thou will	= du wirst.
You people will	= ihr werdest.

I shall play	= ich werde spielen.
I shall study	= ich werde studieren.
He will play	= er wird spielen.
She will study	= sie wird studieren.
They will play	= sie werden spielen.
We will study	= wir werden studieren.

I shall not play	= ich werde nicht spielen.
I shall not study	= ich werde nicht studieren.
Shall I play?	= werde ich spielen?
Shall I study?	= werde ich studieren?
Shall I not play?	= werde ich nicht spielen?
Shall I not study	= werde ich nicht studieren?

We shall not go	= wir werden nicht gehen.
He will not do	= er wird nicht tun. (toon)
She will not answer	= sie wird nicht antworten.
I shall not write	= ich werde nicht schreiben.
I shall not copy	= ich werde nicht abschreiben.
Will you not come?	= werden Sie nicht kommen?
Will you not ask?	= werden Sie nicht fragen?
Will she come?	= wird sie kommen?

I shall do it	
(I shall it do)	= ich werde **es** tun. ['es' is an object. Object comes before main verb]
He will not do it	
(He will it not do)	= er wird es nicht tun. [Use of 'nicht' is complicated-will explain later]
I shall not go out	
(I shall not out go)	= ich werde nicht aus gehen.
They will not copy it	
(They will it not copy)	= sie werden es nicht abschreiben.
I shall write a letter	
(I shall a letter write)	= ich werde einen Brief schreiben.

Lesson 36
Future Pefect Tense
The Future Pefect sentences are formed using shall/will + have. Have = haben is used as a complete verb without chaning termination. And before 'haben' the past participle is used which is the unique system of German language.

I shall have	= ich werde haben
He/she/it will have	= er/sie/es wird haben.
You/we/they will have	= Sie/wir/sie werden haben.
Thou will have	= du wirst haben.
You people will have	= ihr werdest haben.

I shall have played	
(I shall played have)	= ich werde gespielt haben.
I shall have studied	
(I shall studied have)	= ich werde studiert haben.

I shall not have played	
(I shall not played have)	= ich werde nicht gespielt haben.
I shall not have studied	
(I shall not studied have)	= ich werde nicht studiert haben.

Shall I have played?	
(Shall I played have)	= werde ich gespielt haben?
Shall I have studied?	
(Shall I studied have)	= werde ich studiert haben?

I shall have bought	= ich werde gekauft haben.
You will have spoken	= Sie werden gesprochen haben. (geshproshen)
He will have sold his house	= er wird sein Hause verkauft haben. [sein = his]
They will have sold it	= sie werden es verkauft haben.
The boy will have learnt	= der Knabe wird gelernt haben. (knaabe)
We will have waited	= wir werden gewartet haben.
I will have answred	= ich werde geantwortet haben.
Will he have waited?	= wird er gewartet haben?
Will I have become	= werde ich geworden haben?
Will she have answred?	= wird sie geantwortet haben?
Will you have waited?	= werden Sie gewartet haben?
Will she have written?	= wird sie geschrieben haben?

Exercise: -
Translate these sentences into German.
I play. I do not play. Do I play? Do I not play? I am playing. I am not playing. Am I playing? Am I not playing? I have played. I have not played. Have I played? Have I not played? I played. I did not play. Did I play? Did I not play? I had played. I had not played. Had I played? Had I not played? I will play. I will not play. Will I play? Will I not play? I will have played. I will not have played. Will I have played? Will I have not played?

Lesson 37

Imperatives

Imperatives (commanding sentences) are formed using Sie (you) after the infinitive verb.

Sell it (you sell it)	= Verkaufen Sie es.
Do not go (you do not go)	= Gehen Sie nicht.
Come with us (you)	= Kommen Sie mit uns.
Look for it (you)	= Suchen Sie es. (zukhen)
Give them the money (you)	= geben Sie ihnen das Geld.

Come here quickly	= Kommen Sie schnell hier. (shnel)
Let him go	= Lassen Sie ihn gehen.
Show it to me	= Zeigen Sie es mir. (tsaai-gen)
Shut the door	= Machen Sie die Tür zu. (machen zu = to close)
Give me a book	= Geben Si e mir ein Buch.
Send her the book	= Senden Sie ihr das Buch.
Send me the answer	= Senden Sie mir die Antwort. (aantwort)

Go	= Gehen Sie.
Wait	= Warten Sie.
Read	= Lesen Sie.
Sit down	= Setzen Sie sich. (zish)
Get up	= Stehen Sie auf. (aauf)
Put the book in your pocket	= Stecken Sie das Buch in die Tasche.
Place the knife on the table	= Legen Sie das Messer auf den Tisch. (den = accusative 'the')

Placing 'Object' and 'Nicht'

This lesson also requires a proper attention. There is a set of rules for placing object and 'nicht' in a sentence.

If there is one verb in a single clause, the verb comes before the object.

I asked him	= Ich fragte ihm.
I gave it	= Ich gab es.

Where there are two verbs, the second verb is placed at the end of the sentence.

I have done it	= Ich habe es getan. [Object falls before verb]
I have bought the book	= Ich habe das Buch gekauft.

The word 'nicht' is placed at various places. In a simple clause of one verb, nicht is placed at the end.

I do not sell	= Ich verkaufe nicht.
Do they not visit?	= Besuchen sie nicht?

If there are two verbs, nicht is placed BEFORE the last verb.

He will not find them	= Er wird sie nicht finden.
I have not done it	= Ich habe es nicht getan.

Lesson 38
Some irregular verbs

offer	= bieten (beeten)
bend	= biegen
begin	= beginnen
stay	= bleiben (blaai-ben)
break	= brechen
burn	= brennen
think	= denken
hire	= dingen
recommend	= empfehlen
eat	= essen
fall	= fallen
catch	= fangen
find	= finden
succeed	= gelingen
recover	= genesen
enjoy	= geniessen
happen	= geschehen
win	= gewinnen
dig	= graben
hold	= halten
know	= kennen
load	= laden
run	= laufen
lend	= leihen
read	= lesen
like	= mögen
take	= nehmen
struggle	= ringen
call	= rufen
push	= schieben
sleep	= schlafen
beat	= schlagen
cry out	= schreien
see	= sehen
send	= senden
sit	= sitzen
walk	= treten
do	= tun
become	= werden
know	= wissen
wish	= wollen

The irregular verbs do not follow any rule while chaning its past and past participle forms. To see their forms, please look into the dictionary.

Lesson 39
Some Expressions

because	= weil (waa-il)
as soon as	= sobald (zobaalt)
by means of	= mittels (mitels)
inspite of	= trotz
during	= während
how much	= wieviel (weefeel)
already	= schon
however	= jedoch (yedokh)
therefore	= daher
but	= aber
in order that	= damit
on this side of	= diesseits
on that side of	= jenseits
a little	= wenig
nevertheless	= dennoch
than	= als (aals)

Where is my book?	= Wo ist mein Buch?
Where are you going?	= Wo gehen Sie?
Where was your room?	= Wo war ihr Zimmer?
May I?	= Darf ich? (daarf)
Why do you allow him?	= Warum erlauben Sie ihm?
You will catch cold	= Sie werden sich erkälten.
Today, it is fine	= Heute ist es schön.
He was out but she was not	= Er war aus, aber sie war nicht.
I saw him but not her	= Ich sah ihm, aber nicht sie.
There is nobody there	= Es ist niemand dort. (es ist = there is)
Please come here	= Bitte, kommen Sie hier. (bitte = please)
Once there was a man	= Einmal war ein Mann.
Bring me a little butter	= Bringen Sie mir ein wenig Butter.
They are not coming	= Sie kommen nicht.
We knew him formerly	= Wir kannten ihm.
What kind of children!	= Was für Kinder!
What letters!	= Was für Briefe!
Where did he go?	= Wo ging er?
You must not come alone?	= Sie müssen nicht allein kommen.
They must not go	= Wie müssen gehen nicht.
Where is the water	= Wo ist das Wasser?
You are not allowed	= Sie durften nicht.
I have already eaten my bread	= Ich habe mein Brot schon gegessen.
He is as tall as you	= Er ist so gross wie Sie.
What must I ask?	= Was muss ich fragen?

Lesson 40
Some Expressions-2

Good morning	= Guten Morgen.
Good afternoon/good day	= Guten Tag.
Good evening	= Guten Abend.
Good night	= Gute Nacht.
Good bye	= Auf Wiedersehen. (aau weedersehen)
How do you do!	= Guten Tag.
Thank you	= Danke (daanke)
How are you?	= Wie geht's? (gets)
Please	= Bitte
Please give me	= Bitte, geben Sie mir.
Please open the door	= Bitte, öffnen Sie die Tür.
Can I help you?	= Kann ich ihnen helfen?
Will you please come with me?	= Bitte, kommen Sie mir?
I cannot help him today	= Ich kann ihm heute nicht helfen.
I thank you for your help	= Ich danke ihnen für ihre Hilfe.
Thank you very much	= Vielen Dank. (feelen)
Do it at once	= Tun Sie es sofort.
What is your name?	= Wie heißen Sie?
I am glad you have come	= Ich bin froh Sie haben gekommt.
I am sorry	= Es tut mir leid.
It is of no use to me	= Es nützt mir nichts.
I am ill	= Ich bin krank.
That is too much	= Das ist zu viel.
Too difficult	= Zu schwer.
Too expensive for me	= Zu teuer für mich.
Please sit down	= Setzen Sie sich, bitte.
Please give it to me	= Geben Sie es mir, bitte.
You cannot get in	= Sie können nicht hinein.
Come back soon!	= Kommen Sie bald wieder.
Get in please	= Bitte, steigen Sie ein.
What is the matter with you?	= Was fehlt ihnen? / was haben Sie?
Ask him	= Fragen Sie ihn.
Do not ask him	= Fragen Sie nicht.
Do not mention it	= Nicht der Rede wert.
Excuse me	= Entschuldigen Sie. (entshuldigen)
Believe me, it is true	= Glauben Sie mir, es ist wahr.
What is this?	= Was ist das?
May I offer you something	= Darf ich ihnen etwas anbieten?
May I visit him?	= Darf ich ihn besuchen?
What is the matter here?	= Was gibt es hier?

To know the exact meaning of a few words used in these sentences, kindly look into the dictionary. At most of the places in this book, the word 'ihm' and 'ihnen' is written with small 'i' letter to avoid the confusion of reading it as small 'L' letter.

Lesson 41
Some Expressions-3

Take it easy	= Immer mit der Ruhe!
Silence!	= Ruhe!
It does not matter	= Es macht nichts.
Have another cup of tea	= Nehmen Sie noch eine Tasse Tee.
What is he?	= Was ist er?
What are you?	= Was sind Sie?
I have no objection	= Ich habe nichts dagegen.
Get in, please!	= Bitte, steigen Sie in.
Listen to me	= Hören Sie auf mich!
Do it at once	= Tun Sie es sofort.
I am well	= Es geht mir gut.
It seems to me	= Es kommt mir vor.
Do you not like it?	= Mögen Sie es nicht?
I always do it	= Ich tue es immer.
Can you tell me where he lives?	= Können Sie mir sagen, wo er wohnt?
What is the news?	= Was gibt es Neues?
Was there any news?	= Gab es etwas Neues?
Do you know his name?	= Wissen Sie, wie er heißt?
No admission	= Eingang verboten.
No smoking	= Rauchen verboten.
I shall see you tomorrow	= Ich werde Dich morgen sehen.
Take care	= Vorsicht. (forzisht)
Can I rely on you?	= Kann ich auf Sie verlassen?
How long will it take?	= Wie lange dauert es?
No, I do not know him	= Nein, ich kenne ihn nicht.
Yes, please	= Ja, bitte. (yaa)
Help yourself	= Bedienen Sie sich!
Just a moment	= Moment!
What is the time?	= Was Uhr ist es?
It is 11 o'clock	= Es ist elf Uhr.
It is too early	= Es ist zu früh.
Do you like meat?	= Essen Sie gern Fleish?
No, I like fish	= Nein, ich esse gern Fisch.
Please get me a taxi	= Bestellen Sie bitte eine Taxi.
Here is your ticket, please	= Hier ist ihre Karte, bitte.
When does the bank open?	= Wann ist die Bank geöffnet?
Do you know him?	= Kennen Sie ihn?
Will you wait a little?	= Wollen Sie ein wenig warten?
Hello, who is speaking?	= Hallo, wer spricht?
This is Martin speaking	= Hier spricht Martin.
Can I help you?	= Kann ich ihnen helfen?
Thank you very much	= Vielen Dank.

Lesson 42
Introduction

How are you?	= Wie geht es?
What is your name?	= Wie heiβen Sie?
My name is Ryan	= Meine Name ist Ryan.
Where is Suzan?	= Wo ist Suzan?
He was upstairs	= Er war oben.
Why is he not here?	= Warum ist er nicht hier?
This is not his house	= Das ist nicht sein Haus.
Do not ask me please	= Fragen Sie mich nicht, bitte.
What building is this?	= Was für ein Gebäude ist das?
I cannot accompany you	= Ich kann Dich nicht begleiten.
I really believe you are right	= Ich glaube wirklich, Sie haben recht.
Do you want to ask me anything?	= Willst du mich etwas fragen?
I know nothing of it	= Ich weiss nichts davon.
Will you not wait a little?	= Wollen Sie nicht ein wenig warten?
I cannot wait a minute	= Ich kann nicht eine Minute warten.
Shall I help you a little?	= Soll ich ihnen ein wenig helfen?
Where do you live?	= Wo wohnen Sie?
I live in Mumbai	= Ich wohne in Mumbai.
Where do you come from?	= Wo kommen Sie?
I am coming from Delhi	= Ich komme von Delhi.
I am an Indian	= Ich bin ein Inder.
What are your parents?	= Was sind ihre Eltern?
How many bros and sis do you have?	= Wie viele Brüder und Schwestern haben Sie?
I have three bros and two sis	= Ich habe drei Brüder und zwei Schwestern.
Which house do you live in?	= In welchen Haus wohnen Sie?
Where is your uncle's house?	= Wo ist das Haus ihres Onkels?
Here it is	= Hier es ist.
This is too difficult	= Dies ist zu schwer.
May I smoke here?	= Darf ich hier rauchen?
Can I do something for you?	= Kann ich etwas für Sie tun?
When does the next train arrive?	= Wann kommt der nächste Zug an?
Tell me how much it costs	= Sagen Sie mir, wieviel es kostet?
I like to hire a car	= Ich möchte Auto mieten.
Can I change this?	= Kann ich das umtauschen?
Have you apples or grapes?	= Haben Sie Apfel oder Weintrauben?
Give me a little of it	= Geben Sie mir ein wenig davon.
Bring me a little cheese	= Bringen Sie mir ein wenig Käse.
This is very expensive	= Das ist sehr teuer. (te-uayr)
I will call you back	= Ich rufe Sie zurück.
I am sorry for	= Es tut mir leid um
Is there a telephone booth?	= Ist es ein Fernsprechzelle?
Please dial the number	= Wahlen Sie, bitte, die Nummer.
I telephone to her father	= Ich telefoniere ihrem Vater.

Lesson 43
Modal Verbs

können = can
Ich kann zur Schule gehen.
I can go to school.
Wir können zur Schule gehen.
We can go to school.

könnte = could
Ich konnte keinen Brief schreiben.
I could not (no) write a leter.
Wir konnten keinen Brief schreiben.
We could not (no) write a letter.

sollte (zolte) = should
Soll ich dieses Buch lesen?
Should I read this book?
Sollen wir dieses Buch lesen?
Should we read this book?

würde = would
Er würde Kaffee trinken.
He would drink coffee.
Sie würden Kaffee trinken.
They would drink coffee.

müssen = have to, has to, need to, must
Ich muss Computer lernen.
I have to learn computer.
Wir müssen Computer lernen.
We have to learn computer.

musste = had to
Er musste Äpfel essen.
He had to eat apples.
Sie mussten Äpfel essen.
They had to eat apples.

dürfen = to be allowed, (may)
Darf ich rein kommen?
May I come in (straight)?
Darf ich jetzt gehen?
May I go now?

Lesson 44
Self-Introduction

My name is Niranjan Showman.
Mein Name ist Niranjan Showman.

I live in Mumbai, India.
Ich lebe in Mumbai, Indien.

My job is teaching languages.
Meine Aufgabe ist es, Sprachen zu unterrichten.

I have written some books.
Ich habe einige Bücher geschrieben.

I like to read books and watch movies.
Ich mag Bücher lesen und Filme anschauen.

My city is beautiful and rich.
Meine Stadt ist schön und reich.

I have two brothers and no sister.
Ich habe zwei Brüder und keine Schwester.

I am thirty-five years old.
Ich bin fünfunddreißig Jahre alt.

I can speak English and French.
Ich kann Englisch und Französisch sprechen.

My hobby is to visit new places.
Mein Hobby ist es, neue Orte zu besuchen.

Now I want to visit Europe.
Jetzt möchte ich Europa besuchen.

Speaking a foreign language is good for my career.
Eine Fremdsprache zu sprechen ist gut für meine Karriere.

Europeans are great discoverers.
Europäer sind große Entdecker.

Thank you.
Vielen Dank.

Lesson 45
My City Mumbai

Mumbai is a big city of India.
Mumbai ist eine große Stadt in Indien.

It is the financial capital of the country.
Es ist die Finanzhauptstadt des Landes.

I live in this city from twenty years.
Ich lebe in dieser Stadt seit zwanzig Jahren.

Mumbai is thickly populated.
Mumbai ist dicht besiedelt.

People have very busy life here.
Die Leute haben hier ein sehr beschäftigtes Leben.

Mumbai is famous for film production.
Mumbai ist berühmt für seine Filmproduktion.

Many film stars live here.
Hier leben viele Filmstars.

Life is very expensive for all.
Das Leben ist für alle sehr teuer.

There are many beautiful places here.
Hier gibt es viele schöne Orte.

Local train is life-line of this city.
Der Nahverkehrszug ist die Lebensader dieser Stadt.

I like this for its beauty.
Ich mag das wegen seiner Schönheit.

I live here for prosperity.
Ich lebe hier für Wohlstand.

Mumbai is a cosmopolitan cit.
Mumbai ist eine kosmopolitische Stadt.

I like this city for weather.
Ich mag diese Stadt wegen des Wetters.

Thank you.
Vielen Dank.

Lesson 46
Our Country India

India is my country.
Indien ist mein Land.
I am an Indian citizen.
Ich bin indischer Staatsbürger.

Our country is in Asian continent.
Unser Land liegt auf dem asiatischen Kontinent.

Our national language is Hindi.
Unsere Landessprache ist Hindi.

We have our national flag.
Wir haben unsere Nationalflagge.

Hockey is our national sport.
Hockey ist unser Nationalsport.

Tiger is our national animal.
Tiger ist unser Nationaltier.

There are many rivers in India.
In Indien gibt es viele Flüsse.

This is the seventh largest country of the world.
Dies ist das siebtgrößte Land der Welt.

India is a secular democratic country.
Indien ist ein säkulares demokratisches Land.

We have New Delhi as capital.
Wir haben Neu-Delhi als Hauptstadt.

We believe in peace and prosperity.
Wir glauben an Frieden und Wohlstand.

India is an agricultural region.
Indien ist eine Agrarregion.

It has many beautiful places to visit.
Es hat viele schöne Orte zu besuchen.

India has very nice weather.
Indien hat sehr schönes Wetter.
I love my country.
Ich liebe mein Land.

Lesson 47
About Germany

Germany is a country in Europe.
Deutschland ist ein Land in Europa.

Its neighbors are Austria, Switzerland and France.
Seine Nachbarn sind Österreich, die Schweiz und Frankreich.

Berlin is the capital of Germany.
Berlin ist die Hauptstadt von Deutschland.

It is a beautiful city.
Es ist eine schöne Stadt.

It is also the largest city of Germany.
Sie ist auch die größte Stadt Deutschlands.

German is the national language of Germany.
Deutsch ist die Landessprache Deutschlands.

This country has sixteen states.
Dieses Land hat sechzehn Staaten.

Germany has eighty-three million population.
Deutschland hat dreiundachtzig Millionen Einwohner.

Frankfurt is the financial capital.
Frankfurt ist die Finanzhauptstadt.

This city has the busiest airport.
Diese Stadt hat den verkehrsreichsten Flughafen.

Ruhrgebiet is biggest urban area.
Das Ruhrgebiet ist das größte Stadtgebiet.

Volkswagen is a German car manufacturer.
Volkswagen ist ein deutscher Autohersteller.

Germania was the old name of Germany.
Germania war der alte Name Deutschlands.

Now it is a great power with strong economy.
Jetzt ist es eine Großmacht mit starker Wirtschaft.

Thank you.
Vielen Dank.

Writing this book was really challenging to me.
I thank you for learning this much!
As you have reached here, now you need a <u>German to English</u> dictionary.
Start reading the <u>SIMPLE</u> text of German or refer to my next book "Foreign Language Conversation".
If required, now you can do German A1 certified course and ask us the detail.
Reading simple stories and watching videos will also be a great help.
Daily practice on what you have learnt is necessary to stop from falling down.
Expand your reach with confidence and enter the world of German with gradual and continuous move.
Reading, writing, speaking and listening –do all the four things until you find yourself fully strengthened.
To do German A1 course, you can cantact us for further learning.
You have to pass Goethe A1 or TestDaF A1 Examination.

Niranjan Jha Showman
Trainer, Author Physician, Entrepreneur, Filmmaker, Activist
Founder of Cromosys Corporation
facebook.com/cromosys
+91-9561450045
cromosys@yahoo.com
Nallasopara (W), Mumbai, India

Communicate with People

Listen to Them Carefully

Engage in Conversation

Develop Your Style

Read As Much As Possible

Speak Confidently

NIRANJAN JHA SHOWMAN

Founder - Niranjan Jha Showman

Education and Technology Research Center

Patankar Park, Nallasopara (W), Mumbai. +91-9561450045

Education, Technology, Publication, Healthcare, Newsmedia, Realtor, Filmmaking

www.facebook.com/cromosys

Cromosys Publication
Teach
Yourself
German
NIRANJAN JHA SHOWMAN

Cromosys Publication

Teach Yourself French

NIRANJAN JHA SHOWMAN

Cromosys Publication
Teach
Yourself
Spanish
NIRANJAN JHA SHOWMAN

Cromosys Publication

English
Voice
Accent and
Pronunciation

NIRANJAN JHA SHOWMAN

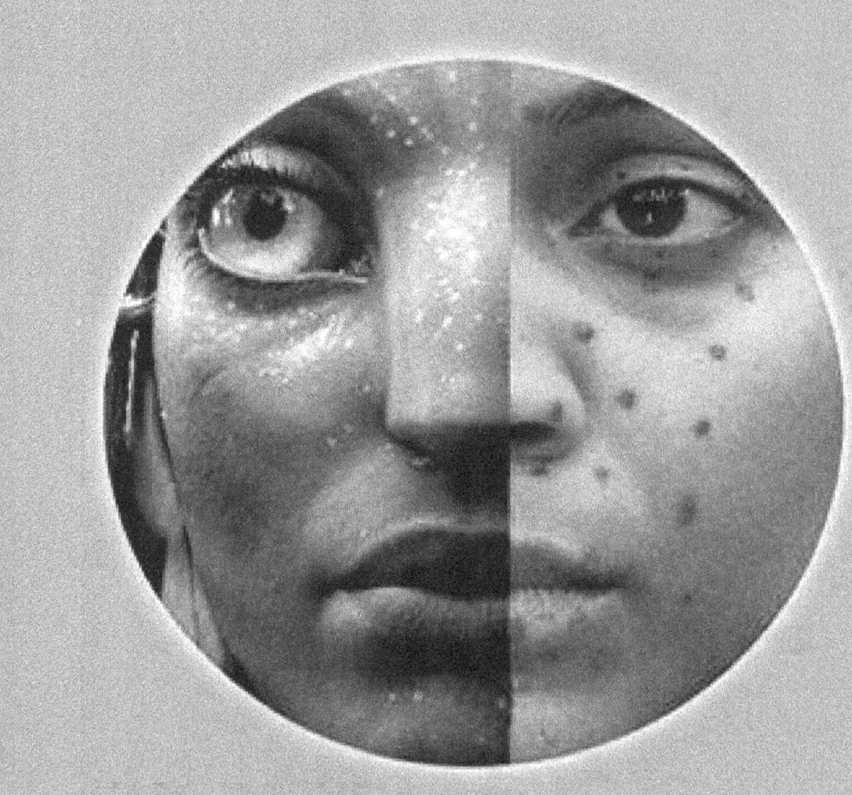

Teach
Yourself
Autodesk
MAYA
Cromosys Publication
NIRANJAN JHA SHOWMAN

Cromosys Publication
Teach
Yourself
Autodesk
3ds Max
NIRANJAN JHA SHOWMAN

Cromosys Publication

CRIMINAL FACTORY

NIRANJAN JHA SHOWMAN

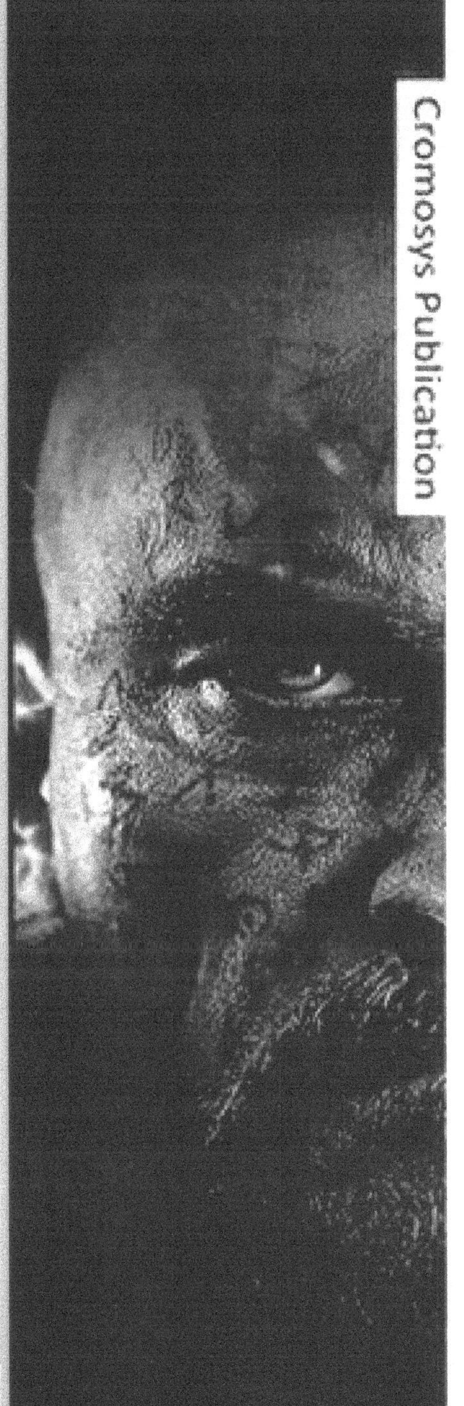

Cromosys Publication

FOCAL DISASTER

NIRANJAN JHA SHOWMAN

Cromosys Publication
Your talents will not help you succeed
without your skill of using them.
NIRANJAN JHA SHOWMAN
BE
MILLIONAIRE
LIKE
ME

Copyright Office
Government of India

सत्यमेव जयते

Extracts
from the Register
of Copyrights

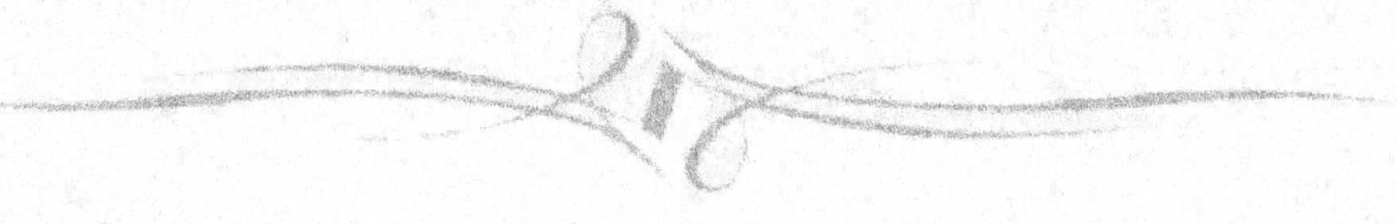

Dated : 24/07/2022

1.	Registration Number	:	**L-76768/2022**
2.	Name, address and nationality of the applicant	:	NIRANJAN JHA SHOWMAN, CROMOSYS PUBLICATION, 001, JAYSATYAM, PATANKAR ROAD, NALLASOPARA (W), MUMBAI, MAHARASHTRA - 401203. INDIAN
3.	Nature of the applicant's interest in the copyright of the work	:	AUTHOR
4.	Class and description of the work	:	LITERARY / BOOK
5.	Title of the work	:	TEACH YOURSELF GERMAN
6.	Language of the work	:	ENGLISH
7.	Name, address and nationality of the author and if the author is deceased, date of his decease	:	NIRANJAN JHA SHOWMAN, CROMOSYS PUBLICATION, 001, JAYSATYAM, PATANKAR ROAD, NALLASOPARA (W), MUMBAI, MAHARASHTRA - 401203. INDIAN
8.	Whether the work is published or unpublished	:	UNPUBLISHED
9.	Year and country of first publication and name, address and nationality of the publisher	:	N.A.
10.	Years and countries of subsequent publications, if any, and names, addresses and nationalities of the publishers	:	N.A. SAME AS ABOVE
11.	Names, addresses and nationalities of the owners of various rights comprising the copyright in the work and the extent of rights held by each, together with particulars of assignments and licences, if any	:	
12.	Names, addresses and nationalities of other persons, if any, authorised to assign or licence of rights comprising the copyright	:	N.A.
13.	If the work is an 'Artistic work', the location of the original work, including name, address and nationality of the person in possession of the work. (In the case of an architectural work, the year of completion of the work should also be shown).	:	N.A.
14.	If the work is an 'Artistic work', whether it is registered under the Designs Act 2000 if yes give details.	:	N.A.
15.	If the work is an 'Artistic work', capable of being registered as a design under the Designs Act 2000.whether it has been applied to an article though an industrial process and ,if yes ,the number of times it is reproduced.	:	N.A.
16.	Remarks, if any	:	

Diary Number :   7393/2020-CO/L
Date of Application :   09/05/2020
Date of Receipt :   09/05/2020

DEPUTY REGISTRAR OF COPYRIGHTS

www.ingramcontent.com/pod-product-compliance
Lightning Source LLC
Chambersburg PA
CBHW041814110726
48006CB00019B/2375